Connections

T0372642

by Scoular Anderson

illustrated by Scoular Anderson

Did you know that inventing spears in the Stone Age led to a series of inventions linking to microchips in computers today? This books shows how - each step of the way through history.

Clever use of stone - Stone Age.

Clever use of stone - today.

microchip

Sharpen a stone

About three million years ago, humans came up with a really clever idea. They began to make tools and weapons from sharpened stone. This time is called the Stone Age.

Over many thousands of years, humans became very good at making spears and harpoons to hunt animals and fish. They made knives to cut up the meat and discovered how to cook it on a fire.

Make some trousers

People of the Stone Age were hunter-gatherers. They were always on the move, living in different places. They had to keep moving to search for animals to hunt and fish to catch. They also gathered fruit and nuts to eat.

People learned how to clean animal skins and make needles from animal bones. Now they could sew the skins together and make clothes. The clothes helped protect them from the weather.

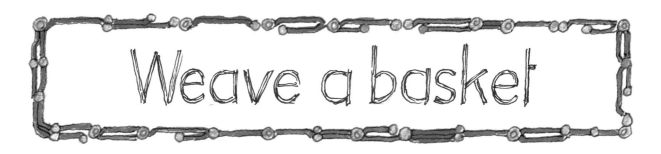

Weave a basket

They had discovered that clothes provided protection.
People realised that they could make things by
collecting thin strips of stuff like ...

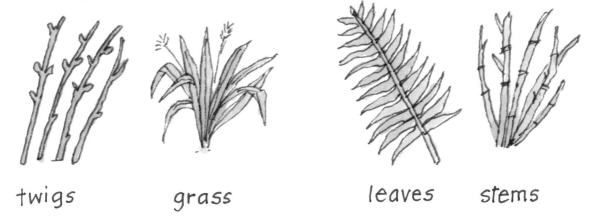

twigs   grass   leaves   stems

... and twisting or weaving them together
in different ways.

They could weave cloaks ...

... or baskets and bags ...

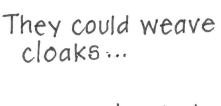

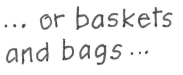

... or ropes ...

... or nets ...

... or even a roof for a house.

7

Keep a goat

This gave people another clever idea. They stopped moving around hunting and gathering. Now life was easier. People kept animals and grew food in one place. They became farmers.

They kept cattle for their meat and milk, and used them to pull carts or ploughs. They also had sheep and goats.

Perhaps someone saw some wool twisted round a twig by the wind ...

... and had another clever idea.

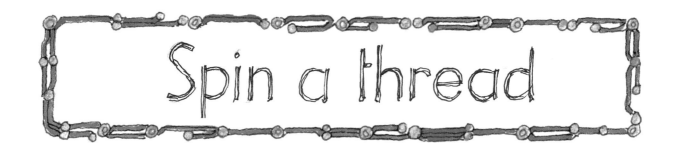

Spin a thread

People began to twist bits of wool together.
They used something called a spindle to do this.
Someone held the spindle and spun it round and
round. They pushed bits of wool towards the
spindle and spun it into long threads.

People discovered they could make thread
from other things.

Cotton came
from a small bush.

Linen was made
from the tough
stems of a flower.

Silk was gathered
from the cocoons of
silkworms (a kind
of caterpillar).

Weave some cloth

Then, the threads were woven
into cloth. This was done
on a wooden frame called a loom.
Threads were tied on the loom
from top to bottom.

A piece of wood called a shuttle pulled another thread
over and under the threads on the loom.

The cloth was
made into
clothes. →

Looms became bigger. Now wider pieces of cloth could be made.

The shuttle went over some threads and under others. This made a pattern.

Weave cloth quicker

About 200 years ago, a man called Joseph Jacquard came up with an idea that made weaving quicker and easier.

He took some paper
with lots of squares on it
and painted a design
for some weaving.

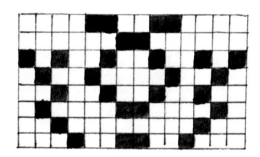

A machine was used
to punch holes in pieces
of card. The holes were
in the same pattern
as the painted design.

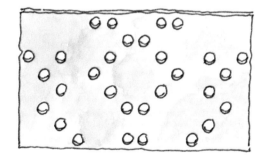

The cards were
tied together in a big
loop and attached
to the loom.

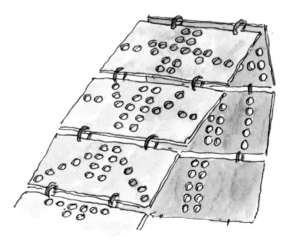

Jacquard had invented a binary system. Binary means that just two options are possible. On Jacquard's card, there was either one hole, or no holes.

The threads on the loom are attached to rods and levers. The rods are pushed towards the cards. If there is a hole in the card, the rods go through and the levers don't move. If there is no hole, the rod bangs against the card and this moves the lever. The lever lifts a thread.

moving cards

These levers don't move.

This lever moves and lifts a thread.

threads

The shuttle passes under this thread and over the others.

This meant that the Jacquard loom could weave cloth into very complicated patterns.

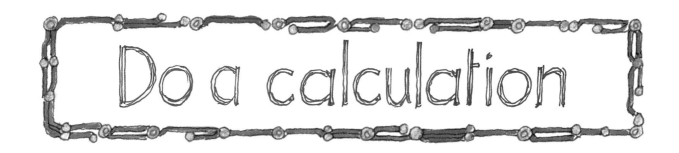

Do a calculation

People have always needed
help to work things out.
They used their fingers
to do simple sums.

Thousands of years ago,
someone invented a way of
working out more difficult sums.
It used beads on wires and was called an abacus.
Working things out is often called 'computing'.

About 400 years ago, a man called John Napier invented another way of doing sums. He had an idea to put numbers on a set of sticks. The sticks were moved around to help with calculations.

They were given the nickname 'Napier's Bones'.

Another invention for making calculations was called a slide rule. It was like an ordinary ruler but with lots more numbers on it. Bits of the ruler slid backwards and forwards to help work out difficult sums.

Turn a handle

Charles Babbage was an inventor who wanted to make machines do much more difficult calculations. His first design had a big handle which needed to be turned. He put numbers on lots of bits of metal. They whirled round and round as the machine did the computing.

Next, Babbage wanted to make an even better machine that would do even more calculations. He worked with a woman called Ada Lovelace. She was a very clever mathematician. They decided they could use Joseph Jacquard's invention of punched cards to work their machine.

Charles Babbage called his inventions 'engines', but they were actually the very first computers. Sadly, he never raised the money to finish building them.

Plug in a wire

Babbage used steam engines to power his machines. When people discovered how to make electricity, machines that did calculations really began to develop.

Inventors designed all sorts of calculating machines to work things out. Many of them were enormous. Some filled a large room!

They were also expensive to make, so only governments, universities and big companies could afford them.

The machines needed lots of people to work the hundreds of valves, switches and wires. If something went wrong, someone had to crawl into the machine and spend days, even weeks, trying to find the fault.

Store some info

Calculating machines became smaller and cheaper. Now, they were called computers.

A computer programmer used a special machine to punch holes in cards. The cards told the computer what to do. Some of them used punched cards to do calculations and store information.

keyboard

card

Other computers used
magnetic tapes
to store information
and do calculations.

Computers became smaller and smaller. Now people
could have a computer of their own at home.

Information
was stored
on floppy disks.

Use a chip

About 60 years ago, microelectronics was invented. This meant that all the valves and switches and wires in computers could be put into one little silicon chip.

All this ...

Silicon is a special type of stone.

... goes into this silicon microchip.

Now, computers could be made even smaller.

Just like Joseph Jacquard's weaving loom, computers use a binary system to work. Jacquard used punched cards with holes or no holes. Computers have little switches that are either on or off – 1 or 0. Electricity whizzes through the computer, turning these numbers into words, sounds or pictures.

When the computer does this: 01100001
you see a on your screen.
When the computer does this: 01000001
you see A on your screen.
When the computer does this: 01100010
you see b on your screen,
and so on.

Get a computer

Today, there are computers in all sorts of things:

... in cars ...   ... in robots that build cars ...

... in phones ...

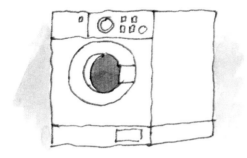

... in washing machines ...

... in planes ...

... in games ...

... in hospitals...

Imagine if nobody had sharpened a stone to make a spear all those years ago. Many of the things we take for granted today – computers, aeroplanes, woven clothes – might never have been invented.

Or perhaps a Stone Age man or woman might have had another idea which triggered off inventions in a totally different way. Today's world would look totally different with a different set of connections!

When did it happen?

First stone tools

Stone Age

Farming

Weaving

Abacus

Napier's Bones, Slide rule

About 3 million years ago

From about 3.5 million to 11,000 years ago

About 11,000 years ago

About 8,000 years ago

About 5,000 years ago

About 400 years ago

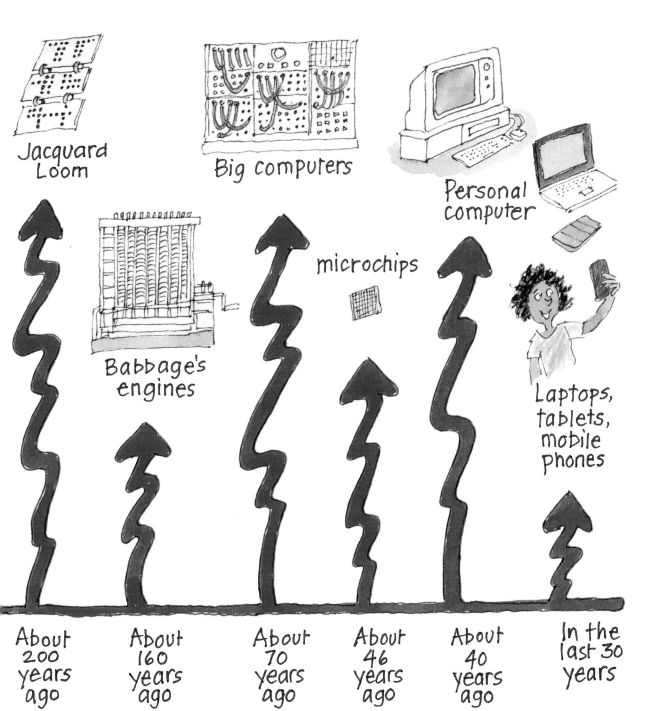

Jacquard Loom

Big computers

Personal computer

Babbage's engines

microchips

Laptops, tablets, mobile phones

| About 200 years ago | About 160 years ago | About 70 years ago | About 46 years ago | About 40 years ago | In the last 30 years |

Index

Author Biography

Scoular Anderson is an author and illustrator of children's books, including picture books, non-fiction, activity books and fiction.

As a child, he spent much of his time writing stories and illustrating them. He studied drawing and design for magazines and books at Glasgow School of Art. He started working as an illustrator at a university in London, and has since written books for many publishers. He particularly loves history. He has written other books for Cambridge Reading Adventures; *Sticks, Bricks and Bits of Stone*, and *Ships, Boats and Things that Float*. Scoular now lives in his home town of Argyll and enjoys gardening and painting.

Connections — Scoular Anderson

Teaching notes written by Sue Bodman and Glen Franklin

Using this book

Content/theme/subject

This beautifully illustrated book explores the path of human invention from the very first stone tools through to the microchips of today's computers.

Language structure

- Appropriate grammatical structures are used, such as the impersonal voice and past tense verbs. (*'threads were woven into cloth' p12. 'People have always needed to work things out'*, p.16).

- Adverbial words and phrases (*'About 60 years ago'*, p.24; *'Now'*, p.25) denote the sequence of events over time.

- Complex sentences are used, demarcated accurately (see p.3, for example).

Book structure/visual features

- Captioned illustrations provide additional information to aid comprehension of the main text.

- A clear logical structure, with additional non-fiction features such as a timeline (pp. 28-29), supports the chronology.

Vocabulary and comprehension

- Clear, simple explanations of technical aspects are given, supported by illustrations (see, for example, p.24).

Curriculum links

History – The book could be used in various different historical topics, comparing aspects of life in different periods and supporting the chronology of change over time.

Computer Science – The book explains early calculating machines and developments in the binary system, which are key components of the information technology curriculum. Work on the binary code can lead to further study of coding, such as historical code-breakers, and the children designing their own codes.

Learning outcomes

Children can:

- consider how text structure and presentation supports comprehension

- identify changes in verb tense, and understand how this supports the chronology of events

- identify unknown words when reading, and use appropriate strategies to ascertain their meaning

Planning for guided reading

Lesson One: Text structure and presentation

Give a copy of the book to each child. Ask them to flick through and to think about what type of text this might be. Draw attention to the non-fiction features (captions, diagrams), and note the use of illustrations rather than photographs – an unusual feature of a non-fiction book.

Discuss the title: *What does the word 'Connections' mean?* Use dictionary sources to establish a meaning, then read the opening paragraph on p.2 which explains the notion of 'connection' explored in this book. Point out that, unlike some non-fiction books they will have read, this book follows a chronology and is read in sequence.

Activate prior knowledge about the Stone Age, and also about computer technology – look at the illustration on p.2, and ensure the children understand the connection here. Go to pp.28-29 and follow the progression from the first stone tools to today's computers.

Go to pp.6-7 to explore the distinctive text layout. Note the use labels, ellipses, and carton-style drawings. Ask the children to read the pages quietly to themselves, and then to tell you what they have learned from their reading. Ask: *Did you find the page layout helpful? Why/Why not?*

Set an independent reading task: to read to p.15. This section leads up to the development of weaving. Remind the children to refer to the timeline (pp.28-29) to track the progress. Remind them to consider how helpful and effective they find the layout of the text in helping them grasp the meaning as they read. For example, you might prompt: *Look at the illustrations here* (on p.14). *They show us examples of the weaving pattern idea that Jacquard had. How do the illustrations help you understand how this worked?*